# A Grammar of the English Tongue

# by Samuel Johnson

# A GRAMMAR OF THE ENGLISH TONGUE.

**Grammar**, which is the *art of using words properly*, comprises four parts: Orthography, Etymology, Syntax, and Prosody.

> In this division and order of the parts of grammar I follow the common grammarians, without inquiring whether a fitter distribution might not be found. Experience has long shown this method to be so distinct as to obviate confusion, and so comprehensive as to prevent any inconvenient omissions. I likewise use the terms already received, and already understood, though perhaps others more proper might sometimes be invented. Sylburgius, and other innovators, whose new terms have sunk their learning into neglect, have left sufficient warning against the trifling ambition of teaching arts in a new language.

**Orthography** is *the art of combining letters into syllables, and syllables into words*. It therefore teaches previously the form and sound of letters.

The letters of the English language are,

| Roman. | Italick. | Name. |
|--------|----------|-------|
| A a | *A a* | a |
| B b | *B b* | be |
| C c | *C c* | see |
| D d | *D d* | dee |
| E e | *E e* | e |
| F f | *F f* | eff |
| G g | *G g* | jee |
| H h | *H h* | aitch |
| I i | *I i* | i (or *ja*) |
| J j | *J j* | j |
|     |     | conson. |
| K k | *K k* | ka |
| L l | *L l* | el |
| M m | *M m* | em |
| N n | *N n* | en |
| O o | *O o* | o |
| P P | *P p* | pee |
| Q q | *Q q* | cue |

| | | |
|---|---|---|
| R r | *R r* | *ar* |
| S s | *S s* | *ess* |
| T t | *T t* | *tee* |
| U u | *U u* | *u* (or *va*) |
| V v | *V v* | *v* conson. |
| W w | *W w* | *double u* |
| X x | *X x* | *ex* |
| Y y | *Y y* | *wy* |
| Z z | *Z z* | *zed* |

To these may be added certain combinations of letters universally used in printing; as, *fl, ff, fi, ffi, ffl*, and &, or *and per se, and*.

> Our letters are commonly reckoned twenty-four, because anciently *i* and *j* as well as *u* and *v* were expressed by the same character; but as those letters, which had always different powers, have now different forms, our alphabet may be properly said to consist of twenty-six letters

Vowels are five, *a, e, i, o, u*.

Such is the number generally received; but for *i* it is the practice to write *y* in the end of words, as *thy, holy*; before *i*, as from *die, dying*; from *beautify, beautifying*; in the words *says, days, eyes*; and in words derived from the Greek, and written originally with υ, as *sympathy*, συμπαθεια, *system*, συστημα.

For *u* we often write *w* after a vowel, to make a diphthong; as, *raw, grew, view, vow, flowing; lowness*.

The sounds of all the letters are various.

> In treating on the letters, I shall not, like some other grammarians, inquire into the original of their form, as an antiquarian; nor into their formation and prolation by the organs of speech, as a mechanick, anatomist, or physiologist; nor into the properties and gradation of sounds, or the elegance or harshness of particular combinations, as a writer of universal and transcendental grammar. I consider the English alphabet only as it is English; and even in this narrow disquisition I follow the example of former grammarians, perhaps with more reverence than judgment, because by writing in English I suppose my reader already acquainted with the English language, and consequently able to pronounce the letters of

which I teach the pronunciation; and because of sounds in general it may be observed, that words are unable to describe them. An account, therefore, of the primitive and simple letters, is useless, almost alike to those who know their sound, and those who know it not.

## OF VOWELS

## A.

*A* has three sounds, the slender, open, and broad.

*A* slender is found in most words, as *face, mane,* and in words ending in *ation,* as *creation, salvation, generation.*

> The *a* slender is the proper English *a*, called very justly by Erpenius, in his Arabick Grammar, *a Anglicum cum e mistum,* as having a middle sound between the open *a* and the *e*. The French have a similar sound in the word *pais,* and in their *e* masculine.

*A* open is the *a* of the Italian, or nearly resembles it; as *father, rather, congratulate, fancy, glass.*

*A* broad resembles the *a* of the German; as *all, wall, call.*

> Many words pronounced with *a* broad were anciently written with *au*; as *sault, mault*; and we still say, *fault, vault.* This was probably the Saxon sound, for it is yet retained in the northern dialects, and in the rustick pronunciation; as *maun* for *man, haund* for *hand.*

The short *a* approaches to the *a* open, as *grass.*

The long *a*, if prolonged by *e* at the end of the word, is always slender, as *graze, fame.*

*A* forms a diphthong only with *i* or *y*, and *u* or *w*. *Ai* or *ay*, as in *plain, wain, gay, clay,* has only the sound of the long and slender *a*, and differs not in the pronunciation from *plane, wane.*

*Au* or *aw* has the sound of the German a, as *raw, naughty.*

> *Ae* is sometimes found in Latin words not completely naturalized or assimilated, but is no English diphthong; and is more properly expressed by single *e*, as *Cesar, Eneas.*

## E.

> *E* is the letter which occurs most frequently in the English language.

*E* is long, as in scē̆ne; or short, as in *cĕllar, sĕparate, cĕlebrate, mĕn, thĕn.*

It is always short before a double consonant, or two consonants, as in *vĕx, pĕrplexity, relĕnt, mĕdlar, rĕptile, sĕrpent, cĕllar, cĕssation, blĕssing, fĕll, fĕlling, dĕbt.*

*E* is always mute at the end of a word, except in monosyllables that have no other vowel, as *the*; or proper names, as *Penelope, Phebe, Derbe*; being used to modify the foregoing consonants, as *since, once, hedge, oblige*; or to lengthen the preceding vowel, as *băn, bāne; căn, cāne; pĭn, pīne; tŭn, tūne; rŭb, rūbe; pŏp, pōpe; fĭr, fīre; cŭr, cūre; tŭb, tūbe.*

> Almost all words which now terminate in consonants ended anciently in *e*, as *year, yeare; wildness, wildnesse*; which *e* probably had the force of the French *e* feminine, and constituted a syllable with its associate consonant; for in old editions words are sometimes divided thus, *clea-re, fel-le, knowled-ge*. This *e* was perhaps for a time vocal or silent in poetry as convenience required; but it has been long wholly mute. Camden in his *Remains* calls it the silent *e*.

It does not always lengthen the foregoing vowel, as *glŏve, lĭve, gĭve.*

It has sometimes in the end of words a sound obscure, and scarcely perceptible, as *open, shapen, shotten, thistle, participle, metre, lucre.*

> This faintness of sound is found when *e* separates a mute from a liquid, as in *rotten*, or follows a mute and liquid, as in *cattle*.

*E* forms a diphthong with *a*, as *near*; with *i*, as *deign, receive*; and with *u* or *w*, as *new, stew.*

*Ea* sounds like *e* long, as *mean*; or like *ee*, as *dear, clear, near.*

*Ei* is sounded like *e* long, as *seize, perceiving.*

*Eu* sounds as *u* long and soft.

*E, a, u,* are combined in *beauty* and its derivatives, but have only the sound of *u*.

*E* may be said to form a diphthong by reduplication, as *agree, sleeping.*

> *Eo* is found in *yeoman*, where it is sounded as *o* short; and in *people*, where it is pronounced like *ee*.

# I.

*I* has a sound long, as *fīne*; and short as *fĭn*.

> That is eminently observable in *i*, which may be likewise remarkable in other letters, that the short sound is not the long sound contracted, but a sound wholly different.

The long sound in monosyllables is always marked by the *e* final, as *thĭn*, *thīne*.

*I* is often sounded before *r*, as a short *u*; as *flirt, first, shirt*.

It forms a diphthong only with *e*, as *field, shield*, which is sounded as the double *ee*; except *friend*, which is sounded as *frĕnd*.

> *I* is joined with *eu* in *lieu*, and *ew* in *view*; which triphthongs are sounded as the open *u*.

# O.

*O* is long, as *bōne, ōbedient, corrōding*; or short, as *blŏck, knŏck, ŏblique, lŏll*.

*Women* is pronounced *wimen*.

> The short o has sometimes the sound of close *u*, as *son, come*.

*O* coalesces into a diphthong with *a*, as *moan, groan, approach*: *oa* has the sound of *o* long.

> *O* is united to *e* in some words derived from Greek, as *œconomy*; but as being not an English diphthong, they are better written as they are sounded, with only *e*, *economy*.

With *i*, as *oil, soil, moil, noisome*.

> This coalition of letters seems to unite the sounds of the two letters, as far as two sounds can be united without being destroyed, and therefore approaches more nearly than any combination in our tongue to the notion of a diphthong.

With *o*, as *boot, hoot, cooler*; *oo* has the sound of the Italian *u*.

With *u* or *w*, as *our, power, flower*; but in some words has only the sound of *o* long, as in *soul, bowl, sow, grow*. These different sounds are used to distinguish different significations: as *bow* an instrument for shooting; *bow*, a depression of the head; *sow*, the she of a boar; *sow*, to scatter seed; *bowl*, an orbicular body; *bowl*, a wooden vessel.

*Ou* is sometimes pronounced like *o* soft, as *court*; sometimes like *o* short, as *cough*; sometimes like *u* close, as *could*; or *u* open, as *rough, tough*, which use only can teach.

> *Ou* is frequently used in the last syllable of words which in Latin end in *or* and are made English, as *honour, labour, favour*, from *honor, labor, favor*.

> Some late innovators have ejected the *u*, without considering that the last syllable gives the sound neither of *or* nor *ur*, but a sound between them, if not compounded of both; besides that they are probably derived to us from the French nouns in *eur*, as *honeur, faveur*.

## U.

U is long in *ūse, confūsion*; or short, as *ŭs, concŭssion*.

It coalesces with *a, e, i, o*; but has rather in these combinations the force of the *w* consonant, as *quaff, quest, quit, quite, languish*; sometimes in *ui* the *i* loses its sound, as in *juice*. It is sometimes mute before *a, e, i, y*, as *guard, guest, guise, buy*.

> *U* is followed by *e* in *virtue*, but the *e* has no sound.

> *Ue* is sometimes mute at the end of a word, in imitation of the French, as *prorogue, synagogue, plague, vague, harangue*.

## Y.

*Y* is a vowel, which, as Quintilian observes of one of the Roman letters, we might want without inconvenience, but that we have it. It supplies the place of *i* at the end of words, as *thy*, before an *i*, as *dying*; and is commonly retained in derivative words where it was part of a diphthong, in the primitive; as, *destroy, destroyer; betray, betrayed, betrayer; pray, prayer; say, sayer; day, days*.

> *Y* being the Saxon vowel *y*, which was commonly used where *i* is now put, occurs very frequently in all old books.

## GENERALRULES.

A vowel in the beginning or middle syllable, before two consonants, is commonly short, as *ŏppŏrtunity*.

In monosyllables a single vowel before a single consonant is short; as *stag, frog*.

> *Many* is pronounced as if it were written *manny*.

---

## OFCONSONANTS.

## B.

*B* has one unvaried sound, such as it obtains in other languages.

It is mute in *debt, debtor, subtle, doubt, lamb, limb, dumb, thumb, climb, comb, womb*.

> It is used before *l* and *r*, as *black, brown*.

## C.

*C* has before *e* and *i* the sound of *s*; as *sincerely, centrick, century, circular, cistern, city, siccity*: before *a, o*, and *u*, it sounds like *k*, as *calm, concavity, copper, incorporate, curiosity, concupiscence*.

> *C* might be omitted in the language without loss, since one of its sounds might be supplied by, *s*, and the other by *k*, but that it preserves to the eye the etymology of words, as *face* from *facies, captive* from *captivus*.

*Ch* has a sound which is analyzed into *tsh*, as *church, chin, crutch*. It is the same sound which the Italians give to the *c* simple before *i* and *e*, as *citta, cerro*.

*Ch* is sounded like *k* in words derived from the Greek, as *chymist, scheme, choler*. *Arch* is commonly sounded *ark* before a vowel, as *archangel*, and with the English sound of *ch* before a consonant, as *archbishop*.

> *Ch*, in some French words not yet assimilated, sounds like *sh*, as *machine, chaise*.

*C*, according to English orthography, never ends a word; therefore we write *stick, block*, which were originally, *sticke, blocke*. In such words *c* is now mute.

It is used before *l* and *r*, as *clock, cross*.

## D.

Is uniform in its sound, as *death, diligent*.

It is used before *r*, as *draw, dross*; and *w* as *dwell*.

## F.

*F*, though having a name beginning with a vowel, is numbered by the grammarians among the semivowels, yet has this quality of a mute, that it is commodiously sounded before a liquid, as *flask, fry, freckle*. It has an unvariable sound, except that *of* is sometimes spoken nearly as *ov*.

## G.

*G* has two sounds; one hard, as in *gay, go, gun*; the other soft, as in *gem, giant*.

At the end of a word it is always hard, as *ring, snug, song, frog*.

Before *e* and *i* the sound is uncertain.

*G* before *e* is soft, as *gem, generation*, except in *gear, geld, geese, get, gewgaw*, and derivatives from words ending in *g*, as *singing, stronger*, and generally before *er* at the ends of words, as *finger*.

*G* is mute before *n*, as *gnash, sign, foreign*.

*G* before *i* is hard, as *give*, except in *giant, gigantick, gibbet, gibe, giblets, Giles, gill, gilliflower, gin, ginger, gingle*, to which may be added *Egypt* and *gypsy*.

*Gh* in the beginning of a word has the sound of the hard *g*, as *ghostly*; in the middle, and sometimes at the end, it is quite silent, as *though, right, sought*, spoken *tho', rite, soute*.

It has often at the end the sound of *f*, as *laugh*; whence laughter retains the same sound in the middle; *cough, trough, sough, tough, enough, slough.*

> It is not to be doubted, but that in the original pronunciation *gh* has the force of a consonant deeply guttural, which is still continued among the Scotch.
>
> *G* is used before *h*, *l*, and *r*.

## H.

*H* is a note of aspiration, and shows that the following vowel must be pronounced with a strong emission of breath, as *hat, horse.*

It seldom begins any but the first syllable, in which it is always sounded with a full breath, except in *heir, herb, hostler, honour, humble, honest, humour* and their derivatives.

> It sometimes begins middle or final syllables in words compounded, as *blockhead*; or derived from the Latin, as *comprehend.*

## J.

*J* consonant sounds uniformly like the soft *g*, and is therefore a letter useless, except in etymology, as *ejaculation, jester, jocund, juice.*

## K.

*K* has the sound of hard *c*, and is used before *e* and *i*, where, according to English analogy, *c* would be soft, as *kept, king, skirt, skeptick*, for so it should be written, not *sceptick*, because *sc* is sounded like *s*, as in *scene.*

> It is used before *n*, as *knell, knot*, but totally loses its sound in modern pronunciation.

*K* is never doubled; but *c* is used before it to shorten the vowel by a double consonant, as *cockle, pickle.*

## L.

*L* has in English the same liquid sound as in other languages.

The custom is to double the *l* at the end of monosyllables, as *kill, will, full*. These words were originally written *kille, wille, fulle*; and when the *e* first grew silent, and was afterward omitted, the *ll* was retained, to give force, according to the analogy of our language, to the foregoing vowel.

*L*, is sometimes mute, as in *calf, half, halves, calves, could, would, should, psalm, talk, salmon, falcon*.

The Saxons, who delighted in guttural sounds, sometimes aspirated the *l* at the beginning of words, as *hlaf, a loaf,* or *bread; hlaford, a lord*; but this pronunciation is now disused.

*Le* at the end of words is pronounced like a weak *el*, in which the *e* is almost mute, as *table, shuttle*.

## M.

*M* has always the same sound, as *murmur, monumental*.

## N.

*N* has always, the same sound, as *noble, manners*.

*N* is sometimes mute after *m*, as *damn, condemn, hymn*.

## P.

*P* has always the same sound which the Welsh and Germans confound with *b*.

*P* is sometimes mute, as in *psalm*, and between *m* and *t*, as *tempt*.

*Ph* is used for *f* in words derived from the Greek, as *philosopher, philanthropy, Philip*.

## Q.

*Q*, as in other languages, is always followed by *u*, and has a sound which our Saxon ancestors well expressed by *cw*, as *quadrant, queen, equestrian, quilt, inquiry, quire, quotidian*. *Qu* is never followed by *u*.

*Qu* is sometimes sounded, in words derived from the French, like *k*, as *conquer, liquor, risque, chequer*.

## R.

*R* has the same rough snarling sound as in the other tongues.

> The Saxons used often to put *h* before it, as before *l* at the beginning of words.
>
> *Rh* is used in words derived from the Greek, as *myrrh, myrrhine, catarrhous, rheum, rheumatick, rhyme*.

*Re*, at the end of some words derived from the Latin or French, is pronounced like a weak *er*, as *theatre, sepulchre*.

## S.

*S* has a hissing sound, as *sibilation, sister*.

> A single *s* seldom ends any word, except in the third person of verbs, as *loves, grows*; and the plurals of nouns, as *trees, bushes, distresses*; the pronouns *this, his, ours, yours, us*; the adverb *thus*; and words derived from Latin, as *rebus, surplus*; the close being always either in *se*, as *house, horse*, or in *ss*, as *grass, dress, bliss, less*, anciently *grasse, dresse*.

*S*, single at the end of words, has a grosser sound, like that of *z*, as *trees, eyes*, except *this, thus, us, rebus, surplus*.

It sounds like *z* before *ion*, if a vowel goes before it, as *intrusion*; and like *s*, if it follows a consonant, as *conversion*.

It sounds like *z* before *e* mute, as *refuse*, and before *y* final, as *rosy*; and in those words, *bosom, desire, wisdom, prison, prisoner, present, present, damsel, casement*.

> It is the peculiar quality of *s*, that it may be sounded before all consonants, except *x* and *z*, in which *s* is comprised, *x* being only *ks*, and *z* a hard or gross *s*. This *s* is therefore termed by grammarians *suæ potestatis litera*; the reason of which the learned Dr. Clarke erroneously supposed to be, that in some words it might be doubled at pleasure. Thus we find in several languages.

Σβεννυμι, *scatter, sdegno, sdrucciolo, sfavellare,* σφιγξ, *sgombrare, sgranare, shake, slumber, smell, snipe, space, splendour, spring, squeeze, shrew, step, strength, stramen, stripe, sventura, swell*.

*S* is mute in *isle, island, demesne, viscount.*

## T.

*T* has its customary sound; as *take, temptation.*

*Ti* before a vowel has the sound of *si* as *salvation*, except an *s* goes before, as *question*; excepting likewise derivatives from words ending in *ty*, as *mighty, mightier.*

*Th* has two sounds; the one soft, as *thus, whether*; the other hard, as *thing, think*. The sound is soft in these words, *then, thence,* and *there,* with their derivatives and compounds, and in *that, these, thou, thee, thy, thine, their, they, this, those, them, though, thus*; and in all words between two vowels, as, *father, whether*; and between *r* and a vowel, as *burthen.*

In other words it is hard, as *thick, thunder, faith, faithful.* Where it is softened at the end of a word, an *e* silent must be added, as *breath, breathe; cloth, clothe.*

## V.

*V* has a sound of near affinity to that of *f*, as *vain, vanity.*

> From *f* in the Islandick alphabet, *v* is only distinguished by a diacritical point.

## W.

Of *w*, which in diphthongs is often an undoubted vowel, some grammarians have doubted whether it ever be a consonant; and not rather as it is called a double *u*, or *ou*, as *water* may be resolved into *ouater*; but letters of the same sound are always reckoned consonants in other alphabets: and it may be observed, that *w* follows a vowel without any hiatus or difficulty of utterance, as *frosty winter.*

*Wh* has a sound accounted peculiar to the English, which the Saxons better expressed by *hw*, as, *what, whence, whiting*; in *whore* only, and sometimes in *wholesome, wh* is sounded like a simple *h*.

# X.

*X* begins no English word: it has the sound of *ks*, as *axle, extraneous*.

# Y.

*Y*, when it follows a consonant, is a vowel; when it precedes either a vowel or a diphthong, is a consonant, as *ye, young*. It is thought by some to be in all cases a vowel. But it may be observed of *y* as of *w*, that it follows a vowel without any hiatus, as *rosy youth*.

> The chief argument by which *w* and *y* appear to be always vowels is, that the sounds which they are supposed to have as consonants, cannot be uttered after a vowel, like that of all other consonants; thus we say *tu, ut*; *do, odd*; but in *wed, dew*; the two sounds of *w* have no resemblance to each other.

# Z.

*Z* begins no word originally English; it has the sound, as its name *izzard* or *s hard* expresses, of an *s* uttered with a closer compression of the palate by the tongue, as *freeze, froze*.

> In orthography I have supposed *orthoepy*, or *just utterance of words*, to be included; orthography being only the art of expressing certain sounds by proper characters. I have therefore observed in what words any of the letters are mute.
>
> Most of the writers of English grammar have given long tables of words pronounced otherwise than they are written, and seem not sufficiently to have considered, that of English, as of all living tongues, there is a double pronunciation, one cursory and colloquial, the other regular and solemn. The cursory pronunciation is always vague and uncertain, being made different in different mouths by negligence, unskilfulness, or affectation. The solemn pronunciation, though by no means immutable and permanent, is yet always less remote from the orthography, and less liable to capricious innovation. They have however generally formed their tables according to the cursory speech of those with whom they happened to converse; and concluding that the whole nation combines to vitiate language in one manner, have often established the jargon of the lowest of the people as the model of speech.
>
> For pronunciation the best general rule is, to consider those as the most elegant speakers who deviate least from the written words.
>
> There have been many schemes offered for the emendation and settlement of our orthography, which, like that of other nations, being formed by chance, or according to the fancy of the earliest writers in rude ages, was at first very various and uncertain, and is yet sufficiently irregular. Of these reformers some have endeavoured to accommodate

orthography better to the pronunciation, without considering that this is to measure by a shadow, to take that for a model or standard which is changing while they apply it. Others, less absurdly indeed, but with equal unlikelihood of success, have endeavoured to proportion the number of letters to that of sounds, that every sound may have its own character, and every character a single sound. Such would be the orthography of a new language, to be formed by a synod of grammarians upon principles of science. But who can hope to prevail on nations to change their practice, and make all their old books useless? or what advantage would a new orthography procure equivalent to the confusion and perplexity of such an alteration?

Some ingenious men, indeed, have endeavoured to deserve well of their country, by writing *honor* and *labor* for *honour* and *labour*, *red* for *read* in the preter-tense, *sais* for *says*, *repete* tor *repeat*, *explane* for *explain*, or *declame* for *declaim*. Of these it may be said, that as they have done no good they have done little harm; both because they have innovated little, and because few have followed them.

The English language has properly no dialects; the style of writers has no professed diversity in the use of words, or of their flexions and terminations, nor differs but by different degrees of skill or care. The oral diction is uniform in no spacious country, but has less variation in England than in most other nations of equal extent. The language of the northern counties retains many words now out of use, but which are commonly of the genuine Teutonick race, and is uttered with a pronunciation which now seems harsh and rough, but was probably used by our ancestors. The northern speech is therefore not barbarous, but obsolete. The speech in the western provinces seems to differ from the general diction rather by a depraved pronunciation, than by any real difference which letters would express.

# ETYMOLOGY.

Etymology teaches the deduction of one word from another, and the various modifications by which the sense of the same word is diversified; as *horse, horses*; I *love*, I *loved*.

## Of the AR TICLE.

The English have two articles, *an* or *a*, and *the*.

## AN,A.

*A* has an indefinite signification, and means *one*, with some reference to more; as *This is a good book*; that is, *one among the books that are good*;

*He was killed by a sword*; that is, *some sword*; *This is a better book for a man than a boy*; that is, *for one of those that are men than one of those that are boys*; *An army might enter without resistance*; that is, *any army*.

In the senses in which we use *a* or *an* in the singular, we speak in the plural without an article; as *these are good books*.

> I have made *an* the original article, because it is only the Saxon *an*, or *æn*, one, applied to a new use, as the German *ein*, and the French *un*; the *n* being cut off before a consonant in the speed of utterance.

Grammarians of the last age direct, that *an* should be used before *h*; whence it appears that the English anciently asperated less. *An* is still used before the silent *h*; as *an herb, an honest man*; but otherwise *a*; as

A horse, *a* horse, my kingdom for *a* horse.    *Shakespeare.*

*An* or *a* can only be joined with a singular: the correspondent plural is the noun without an article, as, *I want a pen, I want pens*; or with the pronominal adjective *some*, as, *I want* some *pens*.

## THE.

*The* has a particular and definite signification.

>     *The* fruit
> Of that forbidden tree, whose mortal taste
> Brought death into *the* world.    *Milton.*

That is, *that particular fruit*, and *this world in which we live*. So, *He giveth fodder for* the *cattle, and green herbs for* the *use of man*; that is, for *those beings that are cattle*, and *his use that is man*.

*The* is used in both numbers.

I am as free as Nature first made man,
Ere *the* base laws of servitude began,
When wild in woods *the* noble savage ran.    *Dryden.*

Many words are used without articles; as

1. Proper names, as *John, Alexander, Longinus, Aristarchus, Jerusalem, Athens, Rome, London*. GOD is used as a proper name.

2. Abstract names, as *blackness, witch-craft, virtue, vice, beauty, ugliness, love, hatred, anger, good-nature, kindness*.

3. Words in which nothing but the mere being of any thing is implied: This is not *beer*, but *water*; this is not *brass*, but *steel*.

---

## *Of* NOUNS SUBSTANTIVE.

The relations of English nouns to words going before or following are not expressed by *cases*, or changes of termination, but, as in most of the other European languages, by prepositions, unless we may be said to have a genitive case.

Singular.

| | |
|---|---|
| Nom. Magister, | *a* Master, *the* Master. |
| Gen. Magistri, | *of a* Master, *of the* Master, *or* Master's, *the* Master's. |
| Dat. Magistro, | *to a* Master, *to the* Master. |
| Acc. Magistrum, | *a* Master, *the* Master. |
| Voc. Magister, | Master, *O* Master. |
| Abl. Magistro, | *from a* Master, *from the* Master. |

Plural.

| | |
|---|---|
| Nom. Magistri, | Masters, *the* Masters. |
| Gen. Magistrorum, | *of* Masters, *of the* Masters. |

| | | |
|---|---|---|
| Dat. Magistris, | | *to* Masters, *to the* Masters. |
| Acc. Magistros, | | Masters, *the* Masters. |
| Voc. Magistri, | | Masters, *O* Masters. |
| Abl. Magistris, | | *from* Masters, *from the* Masters. |

Our nouns are therefore only declined thus:

| Master, | *Gen.* Master's. | *Plur.* Masters. |
|---|---|---|
| Scholar, | *Gen.* Scholar's. | *Plur.* Scholars. |

These genitives are always written with a mark of elision, *master's, scholar's*, according to an opinion long received, that the *'s* is a contraction of *his*, as the *soldier's valour*, for *the soldier* his *valour*: but this cannot be the true original, because *'s* is put to female nouns, *Woman's beauty*; the *Virgin's delicacy*; *Haughty Juno's unrelenting hate*; and collective nouns, as *Women's passions*; *the rabble's insolence*; *the multitude's folly*: in all these cases it is apparent that *his* cannot be understood. We say likewise *the foundation's strength*; *the diamond's lustre*; *the winter's severity*: but in these cases *his* may be understood, *he* and *his* having formerly been applied to neuters in the place now supplied by *it* and *its*.

The learned and sagacious *Wallis*, to whom every English grammarian owes a tribute of reverence, calls this modification of the noun an *adjective possessive*; I think with no more propriety than he might have applied the same to the genitive in *equitum decus, Trojæ oris*, or any other Latin genitive. Dr. Lowth, on the other part, supposes the possessive pronouns *mine* and *thine* to be genitive cases.

This termination of the noun seems to constitute a real genitive indicating possession. It is derived to us from the Saxon's who declined *smith*, a smith; Gen. *smither*, of a smith; Plur. *smither* or *smithar*, smiths; and so in two other of their seven declensions.

It is a further confirmation of this opinion, that in the old poets both the genitive and plural were longer by a syllable than the original word: *knitis* for *knight's*, in Chaucer; *leavis* for *leaves*, in Spenser.

When a word ends in *s*, the genitive may be the same with the nominative, as *Venus temple*.

The plural is formed by adding *s*, as *table, tables*; *fly, flies*; *sister, sisters*; *wood, woods*; or *es* where *s* could not otherwise be sounded, as after *ch, s, sh, x, z*; after *c* sounded like *s*, and *g* like *j*; the mute *e* is vocal before *s*, as *lance, lances*; *outrage, outrages*.

The formation of the plural and genitive singular is the same.

A few words still make the plural in *n*, as *men, women, oxen, swine,* and more anciently *eyen, shoon*. This formation is that which generally prevails in the Teutonick dialects.

Words that end in *f* commonly form their plural by *ves*, as *loaf, loaves; calf, calves.*

Except a few, *muff, muffs; chief, chiefs*. So *hoof, roof, proof, relief, mischief, puff, cuff, dwarf, handkerchief, grief.*

Irregular plurals are *teeth* from *tooth, lice* from *louse, mice* from *mouse, geese* from *goose, feet* from *foot, dice* from *die, pence* from *penny, brethren* from *brother, children* from *child.*

Plurals ending in *s* have no genitives; but we say, Womens *excellencies*, and *Weigh the* mens *wits against the* ladies *hairs.*

Dr. Willis thinks *the Lords' house* may he said for *the house of Lords*; but such phrases are not now in use; and surely an English ear rebels against them. They would commonly produce a troublesome ambiguity, as *the Lord's house* may be the *house of Lords,* or the *house of a Lord*. Besides that the mark of elision is improper, for in the *Lords' house* nothing is cut off.

Some English substantives, like those of many other languages, change their termination as they express different sexes; as *prince, princess; actor, actress; lion, lioness; hero, heroine.* To these mentioned by Dr. Lowth may be added *arbitress, poetess, chauntress, duchess, tigress, governess, tutress, peeress, authoress, traytress,* and perhaps othets. Of these variable terminations we have only a sufficient number to make us feel our want; for when we say of a woman that she is a *philosopher,* an *astronomer,* a *builder,* a *weaver,* a *dancer,* we perceive an impropriety in the termination which we cannot avoid; but we can say that she is an *architect,* a *botanist,* a *student.* because these terminations have not annexed to them the notion of sex. In words which the necessities of life are often requiring, the sex is distinguished not by different terminations but by different names, as a *bull,* a *cow;* a *horse,* a *mare; equus, equa;* a *cock,* a *hen;* and sometimes by pronouns prefixed, as *a* he-*goat, a,* she-*goat.*

## *Of*ADJECTIVES.

Adjectives in the English language are wholly indeclinable; having neither case, gender, nor number, and being added to substantives in all relations without any change; as, *a good woman, good women, of a good woman; a good man, good men, of good men.*

### The Comparison of Adjectives.

The comparative degree of adjectives is formed by adding *er*, the superlative by adding *est*, to the positive; as, *fair*, fair*er*, fair*est*; *lovely*, loveli*er*, loveli*est*; *sweet*, sweet*er*, sweet*est*; *low*, low*er*, low*est*; *high*, high*er*, high*est*.

Some words are irregularly compared; as, *good, better, best*; *bad, worse, worst*; *little, less, least*; *near, nearer, next*; *much, more, most*; *many* (for *moe*), *more* (for *moer*) *most* (for *moest*); *late, later, latest* or *last*.

Some comparatives form a superlative by adding, *most*, as *nether, nethermost*; *outer, outermost*; *under, undermost*; *up, upper, uppermost*; *fore, former, foremost*.

*Most* is sometimes added to a substantive, as, *topmost, southmost*.

Many adjectives do not admit of comparison by terminations, and are only compared by *more* and *most*, as, *benevolent, more benevolent, most benevolent*.

All adjectives may be compared by *more* and *most*, even when they have comparatives and superlatives regularly formed; as, *fair, fairer*, or *more fair*; *fairest*, or *most fair*.

> In adjectives that admit a regular comparison, the comparative *more* is oftener used than the superlative *most*, as *more fair* is oftener written for *fairer*, than *most fair* for *fairest*.

The comparison of adjectives is very uncertain; and being much regulated by commodiousness of utterance, or agreeableness of sound, is not easily reduced to rules.

Monosyllables are commonly compared.

Polysyllables, or words of more than two syllables, are seldom compared otherwise than by *more* and *most*, as, *deplorable, more deplorable, most deplorable*.

Dissyllables are seldom compared if they terminate in *some*, as *fulsome, toilsome*; in *ful*, as, *careful, spleenful, dreadful*; in *ing*, as *trifling, charming*; in *ous*, as *porous*; in *less*, as, *careless, harmless*; in *ed*, as *wretched*; in *id*, as *candid*; in *al*, as *mortal*; in *ent*, as *recent, fervent*; in *ain*, as *certain*; in *ive*, as *missive*; in *dy*, as *woody*; in *fy*, as *puffy*; in *ky*, as *rocky*, except *lucky*; in *my*, as *roomy*; in *ny*, as *skinny*; in *py*, as *ropy*, except *happy*; in *ry*, as *hoary*.

> Some comparatives and superlatives are yet found in good writers formed without regard to the foregoing rules; but in a language subjected so little and so lately to grammar, such anomalies must frequently occur.

So *shady* is compared by *Milton*.

> She in *shadiest* covert hid,
> Tun'd her nocturnal note. *Par. Lost.*

And *virtuous.*

> What she wills to say or do,
> Seems wisest, *virtuousest*, discreetest, best. *Par. Lost.*

So *trifling* by *Ray*, who is indeed of no great authority.

> It is not so decorous, in respect of God, that he should immediately do all the meanest and *triflingest* things himself, without making use of any inferior or subordinate minister.
> *Ray on the Creation.*

*Famous*, by *Milton.*

> I shall be nam'd among the *famousest*
> Of women, sung at solemn festivals. *Milton's Agonistes.*

*Inventive*, by *Ascham.*

> Those have the *inventivest* heads for all purposes, and roundest tongues in all matters. *Ascham's Schoolmaster.*

*Mortal*, by *Bacon.*

> The *mortalest* poisons practised by the West Indians, have some mixture of the blood, fat, or flesh of man. *Bacon.*

*Natural*, by *Wotton.*

> I will now deliver a few of the properest and *naturalest* considerations that belong to this piece. *Wotton's Architecture.*

*Wretched*, by *Jonson.*

> The *wretcheder* are the contemners of all helps; such as presuming on their own naturals, deride diligence, and mock at terms when they understand not things. *Ben Jonson.*

*Powerful*, by *Milton*.

We have sustain'd one day in doubtful fight,
What heav'n's great king hath *pow'rfullest* to send
Against us from about his throne.     *Par. Lost.*

> The termination in *ish* may be accounted in some sort a degree of comparison, by which the signification is diminished below the positive, as *black, blackish*, or tending to blackness; *salt, saltish*, or having a little taste of salt; they therefore admit no comparison. This termination is seldom added but to words expressing sensible qualities, nor often to words of above one syllable, and is scarcely used in the solemn or sublime style.

## *Of* PRONOUNS.

Pronouns, in the English language, are, *I, thou, he*, with their plurals, *we, ye, they*; *it, who, which, what, whether, whosoever, whatsoever, my, mine, our, ours, thy, thine, your, yours, his, her, hers, theirs, this, that, other, another*, the *same, some*.

The pronouns personal are irregularly inflected.

|  | Singular. | Plural. |
|---|---|---|
| *Nom.* | I, | We. |
| *Accus.* and other oblique cases. | Me, | Us. |
| *Nom.* | Thou, | Ye. |
| *Oblique.* | Thee, | You. |

*You* is commonly used in modern writers for *ye*, particularly in the language of ceremony, where the second person plural is used for the second person singular, *You are my friend*.

|  | Singular. | Plural. |  |
|---|---|---|---|
| *Nom.* | He, | They, | Applied to masculines. |
| *Oblique.* | Him, | Them. | |
| *Nom.* | She, | They, | Applied to feminines. |
| *Oblique.* | Her, | Them. | |
| *Nom.* | It, | They, | Applied to neuters or things. |
| *Oblique.* | Its, | Them. | |

For *it* the practice of ancient writers was to use *he*, and for *its*, *his*.

The possessive pronouns, like other adjectives, are without cases or change of termination.

The possessive of the first person is *my, mine, our, ours*; of the second, *thy, thine, your, yours*; of the third, from *he, his*; from *she, her*, and *hers*; and in the plural, *their, theirs*, for both sexes.

> *Ours, yours, hers, theirs*, are used when the substantive preceding is separated by a verb, as *These are* our *books. These books are* ours. *Your children excel* ours *in stature, but* ours *surpass* yours *in learning*.
>
> *Ours, yours, hers, theirs*, notwithstanding their seeming plural termination, are applied equally to singular and plural substantives, as, *This book is* ours. *These books are* ours.
>
> *Mine* and *thine* were formerly used before a vowel, as *mine amiable lady*: which though now disused in prose, might be still properly continued in poetry: they are used as *ours* and *yours*, when they are referred to a substantive preceding, as *thy* house is larger than *mine*, but *my* garden is more spacious than *thine*.

*Their* and *theirs* are the possessives likewise of *they*, when *they* is the plural of *it*, and are therefore applied to things.

Pronouns relative are, *who, which, what, whether, whosoever, whatsoever*.

| *Nom.* | Who. |
|---|---|
| *Gen.* | Whose. |
| *Other oblique* | Whom. |

| | |
|---|---|
| *cases.* | |
| *Nom.* | Which. |
| *Gen.* | Of which, or whose. |
| *Other oblique cases.* | Which. |

*Who* is now used in relation to persons, and *which* in relation to things; but they were anciently confounded. At least it was common to say, the man *which*, though I remember no example of the thing *who*.

*Whose* is rather the poetical than regular genitive of *which*.

> The fruit
> Of that forbidden tree, *whose* mortal taste
> Brought death into the world.   *Milton.*

*Whether* is only used in the nominative and accusative cases; and has no plural, being applied only to *one* of a number, commonly to one of two, as Whether *of these is left I know not.* Whether *shall I choose?* It is now almost obsolete.

*What,* whether relative or interrogative, is without variation.

*Whosoever, whatsoever,* being compounded of *who* or *what,* and *soever,* follow the rule of their primitives.

| | Singular. | Plural. |
|---|---|---|
| | This | These |
| *In all cases.* | That | Those. |
| | Other, | Others. |
| | Whether. | |

The plural *others* is not used but when it is referred to a substantive preceding, as *I have sent* other *horses. I have not sent the same* horses, *but* others.

*Another,* being only *an other,* has no plural.

*Here, there,* and *where,* joined with certain particles, have a relative and pronominal use. *Hereof, herein, hereby, hereafter, herewith, thereof, therein, thereby, thereupon, therewith, whereof, wherein, whereby, whereupon, wherewith,* which signify, *of this, in this,* &c. *of that, in that,* &c. *of which, in which,* &c.

*Therefore* and *wherefore*, which are properly *there for* and *where for*, *for that*, *for which*, are now reckoned conjunctions, and continued in use. The rest seem to be passing by degrees into neglect, though proper, useful, and analogous. They are referred both to singular and plural antecedents.

There are two more words used only in conjunction with pronouns, *own* and *self*.

*Own* is added to possessives, both singular and plural, as my *own* hand, our *own* house. It is emphatical, and implies a silent contrariety, or opposition; as, *I live in my own house*, that is, *not in a hired house*. *This I did with my own hand*, that is, *without help* or *not by proxy*.

*Self* is added to possessives, as *myself, yourselves*; and sometimes to personal pronouns, as *himself, itself, themselves*. It then, like *own*, expresses emphasis and opposition, as *I did this myself*, that is, *not another*; or it forms a reciprocal pronoun, as *We hurt ourselves by vain rage*.

> *Himself, itself, themselves*, are supposed by Wallis to be put by corruption, for *his self, it self, their selves*; so that *self* is always a substantive. This seems justly observed, for we say, *He came himself*; *Himself shall do this*; where *himself* cannot be an accusative.

---

## *Of the* VERB.

English verbs are active, as *I love*; or neuter, as *I languish*. The neuters are formed like the actives.

> Most verbs signifying *action* may likewise signify *condition* or *habit*, and become *neuters*; as *I love*, I am in love; *I strike*, I am now striking.

Verbs have only two tenses inflected in their terminations, the present, and simple preterit; the other tenses are compounded of the auxiliary verbs, *have, shall, will, let, may, can*, and the infinitive of the active or neuter verb.

The passive voice is formed by joining the participle preterit to the substantive verb, as *I am loved*.

*To have*. Indicative Mood.

*Present Tense.*

*Sing.* I have, *thou* hast, *he* hath *or* has,
*Plur.* We have, *ye* have, *they* have.

> *Has* is a termination connoted from *hath*, but now more frequently used both in verse and prose.

*Simple Preterit.*

*Sing.* I had, *thou* hadst, *he* had
*Plur.* We had, *ye* had, *they* had.

*Compound Preterit.*

*Sing.* I have had, *thou* hast had, *he* has *or* hath had;
*Plur.* We have had, *ye* have had, *they* have had.

*Preterpluperfect.*

*Sing.* I had had, *thou* hadst had, *he* had had.
*Plur.* We had had, *ye* had had, *they* had had.

*Future.*

*Sing.* I shall have, *thou* shalt have, *he* shall have;
*Plur.* We shall have, *ye* shall have, *they* shall have.

*Second Future.*

*Sing.* I will have, *thou* wilt have, *he* will have;
*Plur.* We will have, *ye* wilt have, *they* will have.

> By reading these future tenses may be observed the variations of *shall* and *will*.

*Imperative Mood.*

*Sing.* Have, *or* have *thou*, let *him* have;
*Plur.* Let *us* have, have *or* have *ye*, let *them* have.

### Conjunctive Mood.

#### *Present.*

*Sing. I* have, *thou* have, *he* have;
*Plur. We* have, *ye* have, *they* have.

#### *Preterit simple* as in the Indicative.

#### *Preterit compound.*

*Sing. I* have had, *thou* have had, *he* have had;
*Plur. We* have had, *ye* have had, *they* have had.

#### *Future.*

*Sing. I* shall have, as in the Indicative.

#### *Second Future.*

*Sing. I* shall have had, *thou* shalt have had, *he* shall have had;
*Plur. We* shall have had, *ye* shall have had, *they* shall have had.

#### Potential.

The potential form of speaking is expressed by *may, can,* in the present; and *might, could,* or *should,* in the preterit, joined with the infinitive mood of the verb.

#### *Present.*

*Sing. I* may have, *thou* mayst have, *he* may have;
*Plur. We* may have, *ye* may have, *they* may have.

#### *Preterit.*

*Sing. I* might have, *thou* mightst have, *he* might have;
*Plur. We* might have, *ye* might have, *they* might have.

#### *Present.*

*Sing. I* can have, *thou* canst have, *he* can have;
*Plur. We* can have, *ye* can have, *they* can have.

### *Preterit.*

*Sing. I* could have, *thou* couldst have, *he* could have;
*Plur. We* could have, *ye* could have, *they* could have.

In like manner *should* is united to the verb.

There is likewise a double *Preterit*.

*Sing. I* should have had, *thou* shouldst have had, *he* should have had;
*Plur. We* should have had, *ye* should have had, *they* should have had.

In like manner we use, *I might* have had; I *could* have had, *&c.*

### Infinitive Mood.

*Present.* To have.
*Preterit.* To have had.
*Participle present.* Having.
*Participle preterit.* Had.

### Verb Active. *To love.*

### Indicative. *Present.*

*Sing. I* love, *thou* lovest, *he* loveth or loves;
*Plur. We* love, *ye* love, *they* love.

### *Preterit simple.*

*Sing. I* loved, *thou* lovedst, *he* loved;
*Plur. We* loved, *ye* loved, *they* loved.
*Preterperfect compound. I* have loved, *&c.*
*Preterpluperfect. I* had loved, *&c.*
*Future. I* shall love, *&c. I* will love, *&c.*

### Imperative.

*Sing.* Love *or* love *thou*, let *him* love;
*Plur.* Let *us* love, love *or* love *ye*, let *them* love.

### Conjunctive. *Present.*

*Sing. I* love, *thou* love, *he* love;
*Plur. We* love, *ye* love, *they* love.
*Preterit simple*, as in the indicative.
*Preterit compound. I* have loved, *&c.*
*Future. I* shall love, *&c.*
*Second Future. I* shall have loved, *&c.*

### Potential.

*Present. I* may *or* can love, *&c.*
*Preterit. I* might, could, *or* should love, *&c.*
*Double Preterit. I* might, could, *or* should have loved, *&c.*

### Infinitive.

*Present.* To love.
*Preterit.* To have loved.
*Participle present.* Loving.
*Participle past.* Loved.

The passive is formed by the addition of the participle preterit to the different tenses of the verb *to be*, which must therefore be here exhibited.

### Indicative. *Present.*

*Sing. I* am, *thou* art, *he* is;
*Plur. We* are *or* be, *ye* are *or* be, *they* are *or* be.
    The plural *be* is now little in use.

### *Preterit.*

*Sing. I* was, *thou* wast *or* wert, *he* was;
*Plur. We* were, *ye* were, *they* were.

*Wert* is properly of the conjunctive mood, and ought not to be used in the indicative.

*Preterit compound. I* have been, *&c.*
*Preterpluperfect. I* had been, *&c.*
*Future. I* shall *or* will be, *&c.*

Imperative.

*Sing.* Be *thou*; let *him* be;
*Plur.* Let *us* be; be *ye*; let *them* be.

Conjunctive. *Present.*

*Sing. I* be, *thou* beest, *he* be;
*Plur. We* be, *ye* be, *they* be.

*Preterit.*

*Sing. I* were, *thou* wert, *he* were;
*Plur. We* were, *ye* were, *they* were.
*Preterit compound. I* have been, *&c.*
*Future. I* shall have been, *&c.*

Potential.

*I* may *or* can; would, could, *or* should be; could, would, *or* should have been, *&c.*

Infinitive.

*Present.* To be.
*Preterit.* To have been.
*Participle present.* Being.
*Participle preterit.* Having been.

Passive Voice. Indicative Mood.

*I* am loved, *&c. I* was loved, *&c. I* have been

loved, *&c.*

## Conjunctive Mood.

If *I* be loved, *&c.* If *I* were loved, *&c.* If *I* shall have been loved, *&c.*

## Potential Mood.

*I* may *or* can be loved, *&c. I* might, could, *or* should be loved, *&c. I* might, could, *or* should have been loved, *&c.*

## Infinitive.

*Present.* To be loved.
*Preterit.* To have been loved.
*Participle.* Loved.

There is another form of English verbs, in which the infinitive mood is joined to the verb *do* in its various inflections, which are therefore to be learned in this place.

### *To do.*

### Indicative. *Present.*

*Sing. I* do, *thou* dost, *he* doth;
*Plur. We* do, *ye* do, *they* do.

### *Preterit.*

*Sing. I* did, *thou* didst, *he* did;
*Plur. We* did, *ye* did, *they* did.
*Preterit., &c. I* have done, *&c. I* had done, *&c.*
*Future. I* shall *or* will do, *&c.*

### Imperative.

*Sing.* Do *thou*, let *him* do;
*Plur.* Let *us* do, do *ye*, let *them* do.

Conjunctive. *Present.*

*Sing. I* do, *thou* do, *he* do;
*Plur. We* do, *ye* do, *they* do.

The rest are as in the Indicative.

*Infinite.* To do, to have done.
*Participle present.* Doing.
*Participle preterit.* Done.

Do is sometimes used superfluously, as *I* do *love, I* did *love*; simply for *I love*, or *I loved*; but this is considered as a vitious mode of speech.

It is sometimes used emphatically; as,

I do love thee, and when I love thee not,
Chaos is come again.          *Shakespeare.*

It is frequently joined with a negative; as, *I like her, but I* do *not love her; I wished him success, but* did *not help him.* This, by custom at least, appears more easy than the other form of expressing the same sense by a negative adverb after the verb, *I like her, but* love *her* not.

The imperative prohibitory is seldom applied in the second person, at least in prose, without the word *do*; as, *Stop him, but do not hurt him; Praise beauty, but do not dote on it.*

Its chief use is in interrogative forms of speech, in which it is used through all the persons; as, Do *I live*? Dost *thou strike me*? Do *they rebel*? Did *I complain*? Didst *thou love her*? Did *she die*? So likewise in negative interrogations; Do *I not yet grieve*? Did *she not die*?

*Do* and *did* are thus used only for the present and simple preterit.

There is another manner of conjugating neuter verbs, which, when it is used, may not improperly denominate them *neuter passives*, as they are inflected according to the passive form by the help of the verb substantive *to be*. They answer nearly to the reciprocal verbs in French; as, *I am risen*, surrexi, *Latin*; Je me suis levé, *French. I was walked out*, exieram: Je m'étois promené.

In like manner we commonly express the present tense; as, I am going, *eo*. I am grieving, *doleo*, She is dying, *illa moritur*. The tempest is raging, *furit procella*. I am pursuing an enemy, *hostem insequor*. So the other tenses, as, *We were walking*, ετυγχανομεν περιπατουντες, *I have been walking, I had been walking, I shall* or *will be walking*.

There is another manner of using the active participle, which gives it a passive signification: as, The grammar is now printing, *grammatica jam nunc chartis imprimitur*. The brass is forging, *ara excuduntur*. This is, in my opinion, a vitious expression, probably corrupted from a phrase more pure, but now somewhat obsolete: *The book is* a *printing, The brass is a forging*; a being properly at, and *printing* and *forging* verbal nouns signifying action, according to the analogy of this language.

The indicative and conjunctive moods are by modern writers frequently confounded, or rather the conjunctive is wholly neglected, when some convenience of versification docs not invite its revival. It is used among the purer writers of former times after *if, though, ere, before, till* or *until, whether, except, unless, whatsoever, whomsoever*, and words of wishing; as, *Doubtless thou art our father*, though *Abraham* be *ignorant of us, and Israel* acknowledge *us not*.

## *Of* IRREGULAR VERBS.

The English verbs were divided by Ben Jonson into four conjugations, without any reason arising from the nature of the language, which has properly but one conjugation, such as has been exemplified: from which all deviations are to be considered as anomalies, which are indeed, in our monosyllable Saxon verbs, and the verbs derived from them, very frequent; but almost all the verbs which have been adopted from other languages, follow the regular form.

Our verbs are observed by Dr. Wallis to be irregular only in the formation of the preterit, and its participle. Indeed, in the scantiness of our conjugations, there is scarcely any other place for irregularity.

The first irregularity is a slight deviation from the regular form, by rapid utterance or poetical contraction: the last syllable *ed* is often joined with the former by suppression of *e*; as *lov'd* for *loved*; after *c, ch, sh, f, k, x,* and after the consonants *s, th,* when more strongly pronounced, and sometimes after *m, n, r,* if preceded by a short vowel, *t* is used in pronunciation, but very seldom in writing rather than d; as *plac't, snatch't, fish't, wak't, dwel't, smel't* for *plac'd, snatch'd, fish'd, wak'd, dwel'd, smel'd*; or *placed, snatched, fished, waked, dwelled, smelled.*

Those words which terminate in *l* or *ll*, or *p*, make their preterit in *t*, even in solemn language; as *crept, felt, dwelt*; Sometimes after *x, ed* is changed into *t*; as *vext*: this is not constant.

A long vowel is often changed into a short one; thus *kept, slept, wept, crept, swept*; from the verbs to *keep,* to *sleep,* to *weep,* to *creep,* to *sweep.*

Where *d* or *t* go before, the additional letter *d* or *t*, in this contracted form, coalesce into one letter with the radical *d* or *t*: if *t* were the radical, they coalesce into *t*; but if *d* were the radical, then into *d* or *t*, as the one or the other letter may be more easily pronounced; as *read, led, spread, shed, shred, bid, hid, chid, fed, bled, bred, sped, strid, slid, rid*; from the verbs to *read,* to *lead,* to *spread,* to *shed,* to *shread,* to *bid,* to *hide,* to *chide,* to *feed,* to *bleed,* to *breed,* to *speed,* to *stride,* to *slide,* to *ride.* And thus *cast, hurt, cost, burst, eat, beat, sweat, sit, quit, smit, writ, bit, hit, met, shot*; from the verbs to *cast,* to *hurt,* to *cost,* to *burst,* to *eat,* to *beat,* to *sweat,* to *sit,* to *quit,* to *smite,* to *write,* to *bite,* to *hit,* to *meet,* to *shoot.* And in like manner, *lent, sent, rent, girt*; from the verbs to *lend,* to *send,* to *rend,* to *gird.*

The participle preterit or passive is often formed in *en* instead of *ed*; as, *been, taken, given, slain, known,* from the verbs to *be,* to *take,* to *give,* to *slay,* to *know.*

Many words have two or more participles, as not only *written, bitten, eaten, beaten, hidden, chidden, shotten, chosen, broken*; but likewise *writ, bit, eat, beat, hid, chid, shot, chose, broke,* are promiscuously used in the participle, from the verbs to *write,* to *bite,* to *eat,* to *beat,* to *hide,* to *chide,* to *shoot,* to *choose,* to *break,* and many such like.

In the same manner, *sown, shewn, hewn, mown, loaden, laden,* as well as *sow'd, show'd, hew'd, mow'd, loaded, laded,* from the verbs to *sow,* to *show,* to *hew,* to *mow,* to *load,* to *lade.*

Concerning these double participles it is difficult to give any rule; but he shall seldom err who remembers, that when a verb has a participle distinct from its preterit, as *write, wrote, written,* that distinct participle is more proper and elegant, as *The book is written,* is better than *The book is wrote. Wrote* however may be used in poetry; at least, if we allow any authority to poets, who, in the exultation of genius, think themselves perhaps entitled to trample on grammarians.

There are other anomalies in the preterit.

1. *Win, spin, begin, swim, strike, stick, sing, sting, fling, ring, wring, spring, swing, drink, sink, shrink, stink, come, run, find, bind, grind, wind,* both in the preterit imperfect and participle passive, give *won, spun, begun, swum, struck, stuck, sung, stung, flung, rung, wrung, sprung, swung, drunk, sunk, shrunk, stunk, come, run, found, bound, ground, wound.* And most of them are also formed in the preterit by *a,* as *began, sang, rang, sprang, drank, came, ran,* and some others; but most of these are now obsolete. Some in the participle passive likewise take *en,* as *stricken, strucken, drunken, bounden.*

2. *Fight, teach, reach, seek, beseech, catch, buy, bring, think, work,* make *fought, taught, raught, sought, besought, caught, bought, brought, thought, wrought.*

But a great many of these retain likewise the regular form, as *teached, reached, beseeched, catched, worked.*

3. *Take, shake, forsake, wake, awake, stand, break, speak, bear, shear, swear, tear, wear, weave, cleave, strive, thrive, drive, shine, rise, arise, smite, write, bide, abide, ride, choose, chuse, tread, get, beget, forget, seethe,* make in both preterit and participle *took, shook, forsook, woke, awoke, stood, broke, spoke, bore, shore, swore, tore, wore, wove, clove, strove, throve, drove, shone, rose, arose, smote, wrote, bode, abode, rode,*

*chose, trode, got, begot, forgot, sod.* But we say likewise, *thrive, rise, smit, writ, abid, rid.* In the preterit some are likewise formed by *a*, as *brake, spake, bare, share, sware, tare, ware, clave, gat, begat, forgat,* and perhaps some others, but more rarely. In the participle passive many of them are formed by *en*, as *taken, shaken, forsaken, broken, spoken, born, shorn, sworn, torn, worn, woven, cloven, thriven, driven, risen, smitten, ridden, chosen, trodden, gotten, begotten, forgotten, sodden.* And many do likewise retain the analogy in both, as *waked, awaked, sheared, weaved, cleaved, abided, seethed.*

4. *Give, bid, sit,* make in the preterit *gave, bade, sate;* in the participle passive *given, bidden, sitten;* but in both *bid.*

5. *Draw, know, grow, throw, blow, crow* like a cock, *fly, slay, see, ly,* make their preterit *drew, knew, grew, threw, blew, crew, flew, slew, saw, lay;* their participles passive by *n, drawn, known, grown, thrown, blown, flown, slain, seen, lien, lain.* Yet from *flee* is made *fled;* from *go, went,* (from the old *wend*) the participle is *gone.*

## *Of* DERIVATION.

> That the English language may be more easily understood, it is necessary to inquire how its derivative words are deduced from their primitives, and how the primitives are borrowed from other languages. In this inquiry I shall sometimes copy Dr. Wallis, and sometimes endeavour to supply his detects, and rectify his errours.

Nouns are derived from verbs.

The thing implied in the verb, as done or produced, is commonly either the present of the verb; as to love, *love*; to fright, a *fright*; to fight, a *fight*; or the preterit of the verb, as to strike, I strick *or* strook, a *stroke*.

The action is the same with the participle present, as *loving, frighting, fighting, striking.*

The agent, or person acting, is denoted by the syllable *er* added to the verb, as *lover, frighter, striker.*

Substantives, adjectives, and sometimes other parts of speech, are changed into verbs: in which case the vowel is often lengthened, or the consonant softened; as, a house, *to house*; brass, *to braze*; glass, *to glaze*; grass, *to graze*; price, *to prize*; breath, *to breathe*; a fish, *to fish*; oil, *to oil*; further, *to further*; forward, *to forward*; hinder, *to hinder*.

Sometimes the termination *en* is added, especially to adjectives; as, haste, *to hasten*; length, *to lengthen*; strength, *to strengthen*; short, *to shorten*; fast, *to fasten*; white, *to whiten*; black, *to blacken*; hard, *to harden*; soft, *to soften*.

From substantives are formed adjectives of plenty, by adding the termination *y*: as a louse, *lousy*; wealth, *wealthy*; health, *healthy*; might, *mighty*; worth, *worthy*; wit, *witty*; lust, *lusty*; water, *watery*, earth, *earthy*; wood, (a wood) *woody*; air, *airy*; a heart, *hearty*; a hand, *handy*.

From substantives are formed adjectives of plenty, by adding the termination *ful*, denoting abundance; as, joy, *joyful*; fruit, *fruitful*; youth, *youthful*; care, *careful*; use, *useful*; delight, *delightful*; plenty, *plentiful*; help, *helpful*.

Sometimes in almost the same sense, but with some kind of diminution thereof, the termination *some* is added, denoting something, or in some degree; as delight, *delightsome*; game, *gamesome*; irk, *irksome*; burden, *burdensome*; trouble, *troublesome*; light, *lightsome*; hand, *handsome*; alone, *lonesome*; toil, *toilsome*.

On the contrary, the termination less added to substantives, makes adjectives signifying want; as, *worthless, witless, heartless, joyless, careless, helpless*. Thus comfort, *comfortless*; sap, *sapless*.

Privation or contrariety is very often denoted by the participle *un* prefixed to many adjectives, or *in* before words derived from the Latin; as pleasant, *unpleasant*; wise, *unwise*; profitable, *unprofitable*, patient, *impatient*. Thus *unworthy, unhealthy, unfruitful, unuseful*, and many more.

> The original English privative is *un*; but as we often borrow trom the Latin, or its descendants, words already signifying privation, as *inefficacious, impious, indiscreet*, the inseparable particles *un* and *in* have fallen into confusion, from which it is not easy to disentangle them.
>
> *Un* is prefixed to all words originally English, as *untrue, untruth, untaught, unhandsome*.

*Un* is prefixed to all participles made privative adjectives, as *unfeeling, unassisting, unaided, undelighted, unendeared.*

*Un* ought never to be prefixed to a participle present to mark a forbearance of action, as *unsighing*, but a privation of habit, as *unpitying*.

*Un* is prefixed to most substantives which have an English termination, as *unfertileness, unperfectness*, which, if they have borrowed terminations, take *in* or *im*, as *infertility, imperfection*; *uncivil, incivility*; *unactive, inactivity.*

In borrowing adjectives, if we receive them already compounded, it is usual to retain the particle prefixed, as *indecent, inelegant, improper*; but if we borrow the adjective, and add the privative particle, we commonly prefix *un*, as *unpolite, ungallant.*

The prepositive particles *dis* and *mis*, derived from the *des* and *mes* of the French, signify almost the same as *un*; yet *dis* rather imports contrariety than privation, since it answers to the Latin preposition *de*. *Mis* insinuates some errour, and for the most part may be rendered by the Latin words *male* or *perperam*. To like, *to dislike*; honour, *dishonour*; to honour, to grace, *to dishonour, to disgrace*; to deign, *to disdeign*; chance, hap, *mischance, mishap*; to take, *to mistake*; deed, *misdeed*; to use, *to misuse*; to employ, *to misemploy*, to apply, *to misapply*.

Words derived from Latin written with *de* or *dis* retain the same signification; as *distinguish*, distinguo; *detract*, detraho; *defame*, defamo; *detain*, detineo.

The termination *ly* added to substantives, and sometimes to adjectives, forms adjectives that import some kind of similitude or agreement, being formed by contraction of *lick* or *like*. A giant, *giantly, giantlike*; earth, *earthly*; heaven, *heavenly*; world, *worldly*; God, *godly*; good, *goodly*.

The same termination *ly*, added to adjectives, forms adverbs of like signification; as, beautiful, *beautifully*; sweet, *sweetly*; that is, *in a beautiful manner; with some degree of sweetness.*

The termination *ish* added to adjectives, imports diminution; and added to substantives, imports similitude or tendency to a character; as green, *greenish*; white, *whitish*; soft, *softish*; a thief, *thievish*; a wolf, *wolfish*; a child, *childish.*

We have forms of diminutives in substantives, though not frequent; as a hill, *a hillock*; a cock, *a cockrel*; a pike, *a pickrel*; this is a French termination: a goose, *a gosling*; this is a German termination: a lamb, *a lambkin*; a chick, *a chicken*; a man, *a manikin*; a pipe, *a pipkin*; and thus *Halkin*, whence the patronymick, *Hawkins*; *Wilkin, Thomkin*, and others.

> Yet still there is another form of diminution among the English, by lessening the sound itself, especially of vowels, as there is a form of augmenting them by enlarging or even lengthening it; and that sometimes not so much by change of the letters, as of their pronunciation; as, *sup, sip, soop, sop, sippet*, where, besides the extenuation of the vowel, there is added the French termination *et*; *top, tip*; *spit, spout*; *babe, baby*; *booby*, Βουπαις; *great* pronounced long, especially if with a stronger sound, *grea-t*; little, pronounced long *lee-tle*; *ting, tang, tong*, imports a succession of smaller and then greater sounds; and so in *jingle, jangle, tingle, tangle*, and many other made words.

> Much however of this is arbitrary and fanciful, depending wholly on oral utterance, and therefore scarcely worthy the notice of Wallis.

Of concrete adjectives are made abstract substantives, by adding the termination *ness*; and a few in *hood* or *head*, noting character or qualities: as white, *whiteness*; hard, *hardness*; great, *greatness*; skilful, *skilfulness, unskilfulness*; *godhead, manhood, maidenhead, widowhood, knighthood, priesthood, likelihood, falsehood*.

There are other abstracts, partly derived from adjectives, and partly from verbs, which are formed by the addition of the termination *th*, a small change being sometimes made; as long, *length*; strong, *strength*; broad, *breadth*; wide, *width*, deep, *depth*; true, *truth*; warm, *warmth*; dear, *dearth*; slow, *slowth*; merry, *mirth*; heal, *health*; well, weal, *wealth*; dry, *drought*; young, *youth*; and so moon, *month*.

Like these are some words derived from verbs; die, *death*; till, *tilth*; grow, *growth*; mow, later *mowth*, after *mowth*; commonly spoken and written later *math*, after *math*; steal, *stealth*; bear, *birth*, rue, *ruth*; and probably earth, from *to ear* or *plow*; fly, *flight*; weigh, *weight*; fray, *fright*; draw, *draught*.

> These should rather be written *flighth, frighth*, only that custom will not suffer *h* to be twice repeated.

> The same form retain *faith, spight, wreathe, wrath, broth, froth, breath, sooth, worth, light, wight*, and the like, whose primitives are either entirely obsolete, or seldom occur. Perhaps they are derived from *fey* or *foy, spry, wry, wreak, brew, mow, fry, bray, say, work*.

Some ending in *ship*, imply an office, employment, or condition; as, *kingship, wardship, guardianship, partnership, stewardship, headship, lordship*.

Thus *worship*, that is, *worthship*; whence *worshipful*, and *to worship*.

Some few ending in *dom, rick, wick,* do especially denote dominion, at least state or condition; as, *kingdom, dukedom, earldom, princedom, popedom, Christendom, freedom, wisdom, whoredom, bishoprick, bailiwick.*

*Ment* and *age* are plainly French terminations and are of the same import with us as among them, scarcely ever occurring, except in words derived from the French, as *commandment, usage.*

There are in English often long trains of words allied by their meaning and derivation; as, *to beat, a bat, batoon, a battle, a beetle, a battledore, to batter, batter,* a kind of glutinous composition for food, made by *beating* different bodies into one mass. All these are of similar signification, and perhaps derived from the Latin *batuo.* Thus *take, touch, tickle, tack, tackle*; all imply a local conjunction from the Latin *tango, tetigi, tactum.*

From *two* are formed *twain, twice, twenty, twelve, twins, twine, twist, twirl, twig, twitch, twinge, between, betwixt, twilight, twibil.*

The following remarks, extracted from Wallis, are ingenious but of more subtlety than solidity, and such as perhaps might in every language be enlarged without end.

*Sn* usually imply the *nose,* and what relates to it. From the Latin *nasus* are derived the French *nez* and the English *nose*; and *nesse,* a promontory, as projecting like a nose. But as if from the consonants *ns* taken from *nasus,* and transposed that they may the better correspond, *sn* denote *nasus*; and thence are derived many words that relate to the nose, as *snout, sneeze, snore, snort,snear, snicker, snot, snivel, snite, snuff, snuffle, snaffle, snarl, snudge.*

There is another *sn* which may perhaps be derived from the Latin *sinuo,* as *snake, sneak, snail, snare*; so likewise *snap* and *snatch, snib, snub. Bl* imply a *blast*; as *blow, blast, to blast, to blight,* and, metaphorically, *to blast* one's reputation; *bleat, bleak,* a *bleak* place, to look *bleak,* or weather-beaten, *black, blay, bleach, bluster, blurt, blister, blab, bladder, blew, blabber lip't, blubber-cheek't, bloted, blote-herrings, blast, blaze, to blow,* that is, *blossom, bloom*; and perhaps *blood* and *blush.*

In the native words of our tongue is to be found a great agreement between the letters and the thing signified; and therefore the sounds of the letters smaller, sharper, louder, closer, softer, stronger, clearer, more obscure, and more stridulous, do very often intimate the like effects in the things signified.

Thus words that begin with *str* intimate the force and effect of the thing signified, as if probably derived from στρωννυμι, or *strenuous*; as *strong, strength, strew, strike, streak, stroke, stripe, strive, strife, struggle, strout, strut, stretch, strait, strict, streight,* that is, narrow, *distrain, stress, distress, string, strap, stream, streamer, strand, strip, stray, struggle, strange, stride, stradale.*

*St* in like manner imply strength, but in a less degree, so much only as is sufficient to preserve what has been already communicated, rather than acquire any new degree; as if it were derived from the Latin *sto*; for example, *stand, stay,* that is, to remain, or to prop; *staff, stay,* that is, to oppose; *stop, to stuff, stifle, to stay,* that is, to stop; a *stay,* that is, an obstacle; *stick, stut, stutter, stammer, stagger, stickle, stick, stake*, a sharp, pale, and any thing deposited at play; *stock, stem, sting, to sting, stink, stitch, stud, stuncheon, stub, stubble,* to *stub* up, *stump,* whence *stumble, stalk, to stalk, step, to stamp* with the feet, whence to *stamp,* that is, to make an impression and a stamp; *stow, to stow, to bestow, steward,* or *stoward; stead, steady, stedfast, stable, a stable, a stall, to stall, stool, stall, still, stall, stallage, stage, still,* adjective, and *still,* adverb: *stale, stout, sturdy, stead, stoat, stallion, stiff, stark-dead, to starve* with hunger or cold; *stone, steel, stern, stanch, to stanch* blood, *to stare, steep, steeple, stair, standard,* a stated measure, *stately.* In all these, and perhaps some others, *st* denote something firm and fixed.

*Thr* imply a more violent degree of motion, as *throw, thrust, throng, throb, through, threat, threaten, thrall, throws.*

*Wr* imply some sort of obliquity or distortion, as *wry, to wreathe, wrest, wrestle, wring, wrong, wrinch, wrench, wrangle, wrinkle, wrath, wreak, wrack, wretch, wrist, wrap.*

*Sw* imply a silent agitation, or a softer kind of lateral motion; as *sway, swag, to sway, swagger, swerve, sweat, sweep, swill, swim, swing, swift, sweet, switch, swinge.*

Nor is there much difference of *sm* in *smooth, smug, smile, smirk, smite;* which signifies the same as to *strike,* but is a softer word; *small, smell, smack, smother, smart,* a *smart* blow properly signifies such a kind of stroke as with an originally silent motion, implied in *sm,* proceeds to a quick violence, denoted by *ar* suddenly ended, as is shown by *t.*

*Cl* denote a kind of adhesion or tenacity, as in *cleave, clay, cling, climb, clamber, clammy, clasp, to clasp, to clip, to clinch, cloak, clog, close, to close, a clod, a clot,* as a *clot* of blood, *clouted* cream, *a clutter, a cluster.*

*Sp* imply a kind of dissipation or expansion, especially a quick one, particularly if there be an *r,* as if it were from *spargo* or *separo:* for example, *spread, spring, sprig, sprout, sprinkle, split, splinter, spill, spit, sputter, spatter.*

*Sl* denote a kind of silent fall, or a less observable motion; as in *slime, slide, slip, slipper, sly, sleight, slit, slow, slack, slight, sling, slap.*

And so likewise *ash,* in *crash, rash, gash, flash, clash, lash, slash, plash, trash,* indicate something acting more nimbly and sharply. But *ush,* in *crush, rush, gush, flush, blush, brush, hush, push,* imply something as acting more obtusely and dully. Yet in both there is indicated a swift and sudden motion not instantaneous, but gradual, by the continued sound, *sh.*

Thus in *fling, sling, ding, swing, cling, sing, wring, sting,* the tingling of the termination *ng,* and the sharpness of the vowel *i,* imply the continuation of a very slender motion or tremor, at length indeed vanishing, but not suddenly interrupted. But in *tink, wink, sink, clink, chink, think,* that end in a mute consonant, there is also indicated a sudden ending.

If there be an *l,* as in *jingle, tingle, tinkle, mingle, sprinkle, twinkle,* there is implied a frequency, or iteration of small acts. And the same frequency of acts, but less subtile by reason of the clearer vowel *a,* is indicated in *jangle, tangle, spangle, mangle, wrangle, brangle, dangle;* as also in *mumble, grumble, jumble.* But at the same time the close *u* implies something obscure or obtunded; and a congeries of consonants *mbl,* denotes a confused kind of rolling or tumbling, as in *ramble, scamble, scramble, wamble, amble;* but in these there is something acute.

In *nimble,* the acuteness of the vowel denotes celerity. In *sparkle, sp* denotes dissipation, *ar* an acute crackling, *k* a sudden interruption, *l* a frequent iteration; and in like manner in *sprinkle,* unless *in* may imply the subtilty of the dissipated guttules. *Thick* and *thin* differ in that the former ends with an obtuse consonant, and the latter with an acute.

In like manner, in *squeek, squeak, squeal, squall, brawl, wraul, yaul, spaul, screek, shriek, shrill, sharp, shrivel, wrinkle, crack, crash, clash, gnash, plash, crush, hush, hisse, fisse, whist, soft, jar, hurl, curl, whirl, buz, bustle, spindle, dwindle, twine, twist,* and in many more, we may observe the agreement of such sort of sounds with the things signified; and this so frequently happens, that scarce any language which I know can be compared with ours. So that one monosyllable word, of which kind are almost all ours, emphatically expresses what in other languages can scarce be explained but by compounds, or decompounds, or sometimes a tedious circumlocution.

We have many words borrowed from the Latin; but the greatest part of them were communicated by the intervention of the French; as, *grace, face, elegant, elegance, resemble.*

Some verbs which seem borrowed from the Latin, are formed from the present tense, and some from the supines.

From the present are formed *spend, expend,* expendo; *conduce,* conduco; *despise,* despicio; *approve,* approbo; *conceive,* concipio.

From the supines, *supplicate,* supplico; *demonstrate,* demonstro; *dispose,* dispono; *expatiate,* expatior; *suppress,* supprimo; *exempt,* eximo.

> Nothing is more apparent than that Wallis goes too far in quest of originals. Many of these which seem selected as immediate descendants from the Latin, are apparently French, as, *conceive, approve, expose, exempt.*

Some words purely French, not derived from the Latin, we have transferred into our language; as, *garden, garter, buckler, to advance, to cry, to plead,* from the French *jardin, jartier, bouclier, avancer, crier, plaider;* though, indeed, even of these part is of Latin original.

> As to many words which we have in common with the Germans, it is doubtful whether the old Teutons borrowed them from the Latins, or the Latins from the Teutons, or both had them from some common original; as *wine,* vinum; *wind,* ventus; *went,* veni; *way,* via; *wall,* vallum; *wallow,* volvo; *wool,* vellus; *will,* volo; *worm,* vermis; *worth,* virtus; *wasp,* vespa; *day,* dies; *draw,* traho; *tame,* domo, δαμαω; *yoke,* jugum, ζευγος; *over, upper,* super, 'υπερ; *am,* sum, ειμι; *break,* frango; *fly,* volo; *blow,* flo. I make no doubt but the Teutonick is more ancient than the Latin: and it is no less certain, that the Latin, which borrowed a great number of words not only from the Greek, especially the Æolick, but from other neighbouring languages, as the Oscan and others, which have long become obsolete, received not a few from the Teutonick. It is certain, that the English, German, and other Teutonick languages, retained some derived from the Greek, which the Latin has not; as,

*ax, achs, mit, ford, pfurd, daughter, tochter, mickle, mingle, moon, sear, oar, grave, graff, to grave, to scrape, whole,* from αξινη, μετα, πορθμος, θυγατηρ, μεγαλος, μιγνυω, μηνη, ξηρος, γραφω, 'ολος. Since they received these immediately from the Greeks, without the intervention of the Latin language, why may not other words be derived immediately from the same fountain, though they be likewise found among the Latins?

Our ancestors were studious to form borrowed words, however long, into monosyllables; and not only cut off the formative terminations, but cropped the first syllable, especially in words beginning with a vowel; and rejected not only vowels in the middle, but likewise consonants of a weaker sound, retaining the stronger, which seem the bones of words, or changing them for others of the same organ, in order that the sound might become the softer; but especially transposing their order, that they might the more readily be pronounced without the intermediate vowels. For example in expendo, *spend*; exemplum, *sample*; excipio, *scape*; extraneus, *strange*; extractum, *stretch'd*; excrucio, *to screw*; exscorio, *to scour*; excorio, *to scourge*; excortico, *to scratch*; and others beginning with *ex*: as also, emendo, *to mend*; episcopus, *bishop*, in Danish *bisp*; epistola, *epistle*; hospitale, *spittle*; Hispania, *Spain*; historia, *story*.

Many of these etymologies are doubtful, and some evidently mistaken.

The following are somewhat harder, *Alexander, Sander*; *Elisabetha, Betty*; apis, *bee*; aper, *bar*; *p* passing into *b*, as in *bishop*; and by cutting off *a* from the beginning, which is restored in the middle; but for the old *bar* or *bare*, we now say *boar*; as for *lang, long*, for *bain, bane*; for *stane, stone*; aprugna, *brawn, p*, being changed into *b* and *a* transposed, as in *aper*, and *g* changed into *w*, as in pignus, *pawn*; lege, *law*; αλωπηξ, *fox*, cutting off the beginning, and changing *p* into *f*, as in pellis, *a fell*; pullus, *a foal*; pater, *father*; pavor, *fear*; polio, *file*; pleo, impleo, *fill, full*; piscis, *fish*; and transposing *o* into the middle, which was taken from the beginning; apex, *a piece*; peak, *pike*; zophorus, *freese*; mustum, *stum*; defensio, *fence*; dispensator, *spencer*; asculto, escouter, Fr. *scout*; exscalpo, *scrape*; restoring *l* instead of *r*, and hence *scrap, scrabble, scrawl*; exculpo, *scoop*; exterritus, *start*; extonitus, attonitus, *stonn'd*; stomachus, *maw*; offendo, *fined*; obstipo, *stop*; audere, *dare*; cavere, *ware*; whence, *a-ware, beware, wary, warn, warning*; for the Latin *v* consonant formerly sounded like our *w*, and the modern sound of the *v* consonant was formerly that of the letter *f*, that is, the Æolick digamma, which had the sound of φ, and the modern sound of the letter *f* was that of the Greek φ or *ph*; ulcus, ulcere, *ulcer, sore*, and hence *sorry, sorrow, sorrowful*; ingenium, *engine, gin*, scalenus, *leaning*, unless you would rather derive it from κλινω, whence inclino; infundibulum, *funnel*; gagates, *jett*, projectum, *to jett forth, a jetty*; cucullus, *a cowl*.

There are syncopes somewhat harder; from tempore, *time*; from nomine, *name*, domina, *dame*; as the French *homme, femme, nom*, from homine, fœmina, nomine. Thus pagína, *page*; ποτηριον, *pot*; κυπελλα, *cup*; cantharus, *can*; tentorium, *tent*; precor, *pray*; preda, *prey*; specio, speculor, *spy*; plico, *ply*; implico, *imply*; replico, *reply*; complico, *comply*; sedes episcopalis, *see*.

A vowel is also cut off in the middle, that the number of the syllables may be lessened; as amita, *aunt*; spiritus, *spright*; debitum, *debt*; dubito, *doubt*; comes, comitis, *count*; clericus, *clerk*; quietus, *quit, quite*; acquieto, *to acquit*; separo, *to spare*; stabilis, *stable*; stabulum, *stable*; pallacium, *palace, place*; rabula, *rail, rawl, wrawl, brawl, rable, brable*; quæsito, *quest*.

As also a consonant, or at least one of a softer sound, or even a whole syllable, rotundus, *round*; fragilis, *frail*; securus, *sure*; regula, *rule*; tegula, *tile*; subtilis, *subtle*; nomen, *noun*; decanus, *dean*; computo, *count*; subitaneus, *sudden, soon*; superare, *to soar*; periculum, *peril*; mirabile, *marvel*; as magnus, *main*; dignor, *deign*; tingo, *stain*; tinctum, *taint*; pingo, *paint*; prædari, *reach*.

The contractions may seem harder, where many of them meet, as κυριακος, *kyrk, church*; presbyter, *priest*; sacristanus, *sexton*; frango, fregi, *break, breach*; fagus, φηγα, *beech*, *f* changed into *b*, and *g* into *ch*, which are letters near akin; frigesco, *freeze*, frigesco, *fresh*, *sc* into *sh*, as above in *bishop, fish*, so in scapha, *skiff, skip*, and refrigesco, *refresh*; but viresco, *fresh*; phlebotamus, *fleam*; bovina, *beef*; vitulina, *veal*; scutifer, *squire*; pœnitentia, *penance*; sanctuarium, *sanctuary, sentry*; quæsitio, *chase*; perquisitio, *purchase*; anguilla, *eel*; insula, *isle, ile, island, iland*; insuletta, *islet, ilet, eyght*, and more contractedly *ey*, whence *Owsney, Ruley, Ely*; examinare, *to scan*; namely, by rejecting from the beginning and end *e* and *o*, according to the usual manner, the remainder *xamin*, which the Saxons, who did not use *x*, writ *csamen*, or *scamen*, is contracted into *scan*: as from dominus, *don*; nomine, *noun*; abomino, *ban*; and indeed *apum examen*; they turned into *sciame*; for which we say *swarme*, by inserting *r* to denote the murmuring; thesaurus, *store*; sedile, *stool*; ʽυετος, *wet*; sudo, *sweat*; gaudium, *gay*; jocus, *joy*; succus, *juice*; catena, *chain*; caliga, calga; chause, chausse, French, *hose*; extinguo, *stand, squench, quench, stint*; foras, *forth*; species, *spice*; recito, *read*; adjuvo, *aid*; αιων, ævum, *ay, age, ever*; floccus, *lock*; excerpo, *scrape, scrabble, scrawl*; extravagus, *stray, straggle*; collectum, *clot, clutch*; colligo, *coil*: recolligo, *recoil*; severo, *swear*; stridulus, *shrill*; procurator, *proxy*; pulso, *to push*; calamus, *a quill*; impetere, *to impeach*; augeo, auxi, *wax*; and vanesco, vanui, *wane*; syllabare, *to spell*; puteus, *pit*; granum, *corn*; comprimo, *cramp, crump, crumple, crinkle*.

Some may seem harsher, yet may not be rejected, for it at least appears, that some of them are derived from proper names, and there are others whose etymology is acknowledged by every body; as, Alexander, *Elick, Scander, Sander, Sandy, Sanny*; Elizabetha, *Elizabeth, Elisabeth, Betty, Bess*; Margareta, *Margaret, Marget, Meg, Peg*; Maria, *Mary, Mal, Pal, Malkin, Mawkin, Mawkes*; Mathæus, *Mattha, Matthew*; Martha, *Mat, Pat*; Gulielmus, *Wilhelmus, Girolamo, Guillaume, William, Will, Bill, Wilkin, Wicken, Wicks, Weeks*.

Thus cariophyllus, flos; gerofilo, Italian, giriflee, gilofer, French, *gilliflower*, which the vulgar call *julyflower*, as if derived from the month *July*; petroselinum, *parsley*; portulaca, *purslain*; cydonium, *quince*; cydoniatum, *quiddeny*; persicum, *peach*; eruca, *eruke*, which they corrupt to *earwig*, as if it took its name from the ear; annulus geminus, *a gimmal*, or *gimbal-ring*; and thus the word *gimbal* or *jumbal* is transferred to other things thus interwoven; quelques choses, *kickshaws*. Since the origin of these, and many others, however forced, is evident, it ought to appear no wonder to any one if the ancients have thus disfigured many, especially as they so much affected monosyllables; and, to make the sound the softer, took this liberty of maiming, taking away, changing, transposing, and softening them.

But while we derive these from the Latin, I do not mean to say, that many of them did not immediately come to us from the Saxon, Danish, Dutch, and Teutonick languages, and other dialects; and some taken more lately from the French or Italians, or Spaniards.

The same word, according to its different significations, often has a different origin; as, *to bear a burden*, from *fero*; but *to bear*, whence *birth*, *born*, *bairn*, comes from *pario*; and *a bear*, at least if it be of Latin original, from *fera*. Thus *perch*, a fish, from *perca*; but *perch*, a measure, from *pertica*, and likewise *to perch*. To *spell* is from *syllaba*; but *spell*, an inchantment, by which it is believed that the boundaries are so fixed in lands that none can pass them against the master's will, from *expello*; and *spell*, a messenger, from *epistola*; whence *gospel*, *good-spell*, or *god-spell*. Thus *freese*, or *freeze*, from *frigesco*; but *freeze*, an architectonick word, from *zophorus*; but *freeze*, for *cloth*, from *Frisia*, or perhaps from *frigesco*, as being more fit than any other for keeping out the cold.

There are many words among us, even monosyllables, compounded of two or more words, at least serving instead of compounds, and comprising the signification of more words that one; as, from *scrip* and *roll* comes *scroll*; from *proud* and *dance*, *prance*; from *st* of the verb *stay* or *stand* and *out*, is made *stout*; from *stout* and *hardy*, *sturdy*; from *sp* of *spit* or *spew*, and *out*, comes *spout*; from the same *sp* with the termination *in*, is *spin*; and adding *out*, *spin out*: and from the same *sp*, with it, is *spit*, which only differs from *spout* in that it is smaller, and with less noise and force; but *sputter* is, because of the obscure *u*, something between *spit* and *spout*: and by reason of adding *r*, it intimates a frequent iteration and noise, but obscurely confused; whereas *spatter*, on account of the sharper and clearer vowel *a*, intimates a more distinct poise, in which it chiefly differs from *sputter*. From the same *sp* and the termination *ark*, comes *spark*, signifying a single emission of fire with a noise; namely *sp*, the emission, *ar*, the more acute noise, and *k*, the mute consonant, intimates its being suddenly terminated; but adding *l*, is made the frequentative *sparkle*. The same *sp*, by adding *r*, that is *spr*, implies a more lively impetus of diffusing or expanding itself; to which adding the termination *ing*, it becomes *spring*: its vigour *spr* imports; its sharpness the termination *ing*; and lastly *in* acute and tremulous, ending in the mute consonant *g*, denotes the sudden ending of any motion, that it is meant in its primary signification, of a single, not a complicated exilition. Hence we call *spring* whatever has an elastick force; as also a fountain of water, and thence the origin of any thing: and to *spring*, to germinate, and *spring*, one of the four seasons. From the same *spr* and *out*, is formed sprout, and wit the termination *ig*, *sprig*; of which the following, for the most part, is the difference: *sprout*, of a grosser sound, imports a fatter or grosser bud; *sprig*, of a slenderer sound, denotes a smaller shoot. In like manner, from *str* of the verb *strive*, and *out*, comes *strout*, and *strut*. From the same *str*, and the termination *uggle*, is made *struggle*; and this *gl* imports, but without any great noise, by reason of the obscure sound of the vowel *u*. In like manner, from *throw* and *roll* is made *troll*, and almost in the same sense is *trundle*, from *throw* or *thrust*, and *rundle*. Thus *graff* or *grough* is compounded of *grave* and *rough*; and *trudge* from *tread* or *trot*, and *drudge*.

In these observations it is easy to discover great sagacity and great extravagance, an ability to do much defeated by the desire of doing more than enough. It may be remarked,

1. That Wallis's derivations are often so made, that by the same license any language may be deduced from any other.

2. That he makes no distinction between words immediately derived by us from the Latin, and those which being copied from other languages, can therefore afford no example of the genius of the English language, or its laws of derivation.

3. That he derives from the Latin, often with great harshness and violence, words apparently Teutonick; and therefore, according to his own declaration, probably older than the tongue to which he refers them.

4. That some of his derivations are apparently erroneous.

## SYNTAX.

> The established practice of grammarians requires that I should here treat of the Syntax; but our language has so little inflection, or variety of terminations, that its construction neither requires nor admits many rules. Wallis, therefore, has totally neglected it; and Jonson, whose desire of following the writers upon the learned languages made him think a syntax indispensably necessary, has published such petty observations as were better omitted.

The verb, as in other languages, agrees with the nominative in number and person; as, *Thou fliest from good*; *He runs to death*.

Our adjectives and pronouns are invariable.

Of two substantives the noun possessive is in the genitive; as, *His father's glory*; *The sun's heat*.

Verbs transitive require an oblique case; as, *He loves me*; *You fear him*.

All prepositions require an oblique case: as, *He gave this* to *me*; *He took this* from *me*; *He says this* of *me*; *He came* with *me*.

# PROSODY.

It is common for those that deliver the grammar of modern languages, to omit the Prosody. So that of the Italians is neglected by Buomattei; that of the French by Desmarais; aad that of the English by Wallis, Cooper, and even by Jonson, though a poet. But as the laws of metre are included in the idea of grammar, I have thought proper to insert them.

PROSODY comprises *orthoepy*, or the rules of pronunciation; and *orthometry*, or the laws of versification.

*Pronunciation* is just, when every letter has its proper sound, and every syllable has its proper accent, or, which in English versification is the same, its proper quantity.

The sounds of the letters have been already explained; and rules for the accent or quantity are not easily to be given, being subject to innumerable exceptions. Such, however, as I have read or formed, I shall here propose.

1. Of dissyllables, formed by affixing a termination, the former syllable is commonly accented, as *chíldish, kíngdom, áctest, ácted, tóilsome, lóver, scóffer, faírer, fóremost, zéalous, fúlness, gódly, meékly, ártist.*

2. Dissyllables formed by prefixing a syllable to the radical word, have commonly the accent on the latter; as to *begét*, to *beseém*, to *bestów*.

3. Of dissyllables, which are at once nouns and verbs, the verb has commonly the accent on the latter, and the noun on the former syllable; as, *to descánt, a déscant; to cemént, a cément; to contráct, a cóntract.*

This rule has many exceptions. Though verbs seldom have their accent on the former, yet nouns often have it on the latter syllable; as *delíght, perfúme*.

4. All dissyllables ending in *y*, as *cránny*; in *our*, as *lábour, fávour*; in *ow*, as *wíllow, wállow*, except *allów*; in *le*, as *báttle, bíble*; in *ish*, as *bánish*; in *ck*, as *cámbrick, cássock*; in *ter*, as *to bátter*; in *age*, as *coúrage*, in *en*, as *fásten*; in *et*, as *quíet*; accent the former syllable.

5. Dissyllable nouns in *er*, as *cánker, bútter*, have the accent on the former syllable.

6. Dissyllable verbs terminating in a consonant and *e* final, as *comprise, escápe*; or having a diphthong in the last syllable, as *appéase, revéal*; or ending in two consonants, as *atténd*; have the accent on the latter syllable.

7. Dissyllable nouns having a diphthong in the latter syllable, have commonly their accent on the latter syllable, as *appláuse*; except words in *ain, cértain, moúntain*.

8. Trissyllables formed by adding a termination, or prefixing a syllable, retain the accent of the radical word; as, *lóveliness, ténderness, contémner, wágonner, phýsical, bespátter, cómmenting, comménding, assúrance*.

9. Trissyllables ending in *ous*, as *grácious, árduous*; in *al*, as *cápital*; in *ion*, as *méntion*; accent the first.

10. Trissyllables ending in *ce, ent*, and *ate*, accent the first syllable, as *cóuntenance, cóntinence, ármament, ímminent, élegant, própagate*, except they be derived from words having the accent on the last, as *connívance, acquáintance*; or the middle syllable hath a vowel before two consonants, as *promúlgate*.

11. Trissyllables ending in *y*, as *éntity, spécify, líberty, víctory, súbsidy*, commonly accent the first syllable.

12. Trissyllables in *re* or *le* accent the first syllable, as *légible, théatre*, except *discíple*, and some words which have a position, as *exámple, epístle*.

13. Trissyllables in *ude* commonly accent the first syllable, as *plénitude*.

14. Trissyllables ending in *ator* or *atour*, as *creátour*; or having in the middle syllable a diphthong, as *endeávour*; or a vowel before two consonants, as *doméstick*; accent the middle syllable.

15. Trissyllables that have their accent on the last syllable are commonly French, as *acquiésce, repartée, magazíne*, or words formed by prefixing one or two syllables to an acute syllable, as *immatúre, overchárge*.

16. Polysyllables, or words of more than three syllables, follow the accent of the words from which they are derived, as *árrogating, cóntinency, incóntinently, comméndable, commúnicableness*. We should therefore say

*dispútable, indispútable*; rather than *dísputable, indísputable*; and *advertísement*, rather than *advértisement*.

17. Words in *ion* have the accent upon the antepenult, as *salvátion, perturbátion, concóction*; words in *atour* or *ator* on the penult, as *dedicátor*.

18. Words ending in *le* commonly have the accent on the first syllable, as *ámicable,* unless the second syllable have a vowel before two consonants, as *combústible.*

19. Words ending in *ous* have the accents on the antepenult, as *uxórious, volúptuous.*

20. Words ending in *ty* have their accent on the antepenult, as *pusillanímity, actívity.*

> These rules are not advanced as complete or infallible, but proposed as useful. Almost every rule of every language has its exceptions; and in English, as in other tongues, much must be learned by example and authority. Perhaps more and better rules may be given that have escaped my observation.

VERSIFICATION is the arrangement of a certain number of syllables according to certain laws.

The feet of our verses are either iambick, as *alóft, creáte*; or trochaick, as *hóly, lófty.*

Our iambick measure comprises verses

Of four syllables,

Most good, most fair,
Or things as rare,
To call you's lost;
For all the cost
Words can bestow,
So poorly show
Upon your praise,
That all the ways
Sense hath, come short.        *Drayton.*

With ravish'd ears

The monarch hears.        *Dryden.*

Of six,

This while we are abroad,
   Shall we not touch our lyre?
Shall we not sing an ode?
   Or shall that holy fire,
In us that strongly glow'd,
   In this cold air expire?

Though in the utmost peak,
   A while we do remain,
Amongst the mountains bleak,
   Expos'd to sleet and rain,
No sport our hours shall break,
   To exercise our vein.

What though bright Phœbus' beams
   Refresh the southern ground,
And though the princely Thames
   With beauteous nymphs abound,
And by old Camber's streams
   Be many wonders found:

Yet many rivers clear
   Here glide in silver swathes,
And what of all most dear,
   Buxton's delicious baths,
Strong ale and noble chear,
   T' asswage breem winters scathes.

In places far or near,
   Or famous, or obscure,
Where wholsom is the air,
   Or where the most impure,
All times, and every where,
   The muse is still in ure.        *Drayton.*

Of eight, which is the usual measure for short poems,

And may at last my weary age
Find out the peaceful hermitage,
The hairy gown, and mossy cell,
Where I may sit, and nightly spell
Of ev'ry star the sky doth shew,
And ev'ry herb that sips the dew.　　　*Milton.*

Of ten, which is the common measure of heroick and tragick poetry,

Full in the midst of this created space,
Betwixt heav'n, earth, and skies, there stands a place
Confining on all three; with triple bound;
Whence all things, though remote, are view'd around,
And thither bring their undulating sound.
The palace of loud Fame, her seat of pow'r,
Plac'd on the summit of a lofty tow'r;
A thousand winding entries long and wide
Receive of fresh reports a flowing tide.
A thousand crannies in the walls are made;
Nor gate nor bars exclude the busy trade.
Tis built of brass, the better to diffuse
The spreading sounds, and multiply the news;
Where echoes in repeated echoes play:
A mart for ever full; and open night and day.
Nor silence is within, nor voice express,
But a deaf noise of sounds that never cease;
Confus'd and chiding, like the hollow roar
Of tides, receding from th' insulted shore;
Or like the broken thunder heard from far,
When Jove to distance drives the rolling war.
The courts are fill'd with a tumultuous din,
Of crouds, or issuing forth, or ent'ring in:
A thorough-fare of news; where some devise
Things never heard, some mingle truth with lies:
The troubled air with empty sounds they beat,

Intent to hear, and eager to repeat.      *Dryden.*

In all these measures the accents are to be placed on even syllables; and every line considered by itself is more harmonious, as this rule is more strictly observed. The variations necessary to pleasure belong to the art of poetry, not the rules of grammar.

Our trochaick measures are Of three syllables,

Here we may
Think and pray,
Before death
Stops our breath:
Other joys
Are but toys.      *Walton's Angler.*

Of five,

In the days of old,
Stories plainly told,
Lovers felt annoy.      *Old Ballad.*

Of seven,

Fairest piece of well form'd earth,
Urge not thus your haughty birth.      *Waller.*

In these measures the accent is to be placed on the odd syllables.

These are the measures which are now in use, and above the rest those of seven, eight, and ten syllables. Our ancient poets wrote verses sometimes of twelve syllables, as Drayton's Polyolbion.

Of all the Cambrian shires their heads that bear so high,
And farth'st survey their soils with an ambitious eye,
Mervinia for her hills, as for their matchless crouds,
The nearest that are said to kiss the wand'ring clouds,
Especial audience craves, offended with the throng,
That she of all the rest neglected was so long;

Alledging for herself, when, through the Saxons' pride,
The godlike race of Brute to Severn's setting side
Were cruelly inforc'd, her mountains did relieve
Those whom devouring war else every where did grieve.
And when all Wales beside (by fortune or by might)
Unto her ancient foe resign'd her ancient right,
A constant maiden still she only did remain,
The last her genuine laws which stoutly did retain.
And as each one is prais'd for her peculiar things;
So only she is rich, in mountains, meres and springs,
And holds herself as great in her superfluous waste,
As others by their towns, and fruitful tillage grac'd.

And of fourteen, as Chapman's Homer.

And as the mind of such a man, that hath a long way gone,
And either knoweth not his way, or else would let alone,
His purpos'd journey, is distract.

The measures of twelve and fourteen syllables were often mingled by our old poets, sometimes in alternate lines, and sometimes in alternate couplets.

The verse of twelve syllables, called an *Alexandrine*, is now only used to diversify heroick lines.

Waller was smooth, but Dryden taught to join
The varying verse, the full resounding line,
The long majestick march, and energy divine.        *Pope.*

The pause in the Alexandrine must be at the sixth syllable.

The verse of fourteen syllables is now broken into a soft lyrick measure of verses, consisting alternately of eight syllables and six.

She to receive thy radiant name,
    Selects a whiter space.        *Fenton.*

When all shall praise, and ev'ry lay
    Devote a wreath to thee,

That day, for come it will, that day
   Shall I lament to see.     *Lewis to Pope.*

Beneath this tomb an infant lies
   To earth whose body lent,
Hereafter shall more glorious rise,
   But not more innocent.
When the Archangel's trump shall blow,
   And souls to bodies join,
What crowds shall wish their lives below
   Had been as short as thine!    *Wesley.*

We have another measure very quick and lively, and therefore much used in songs, which may be called the *anapestick*, in which the accent rests upon every third syllable.

May I góvern my pássions with ábsolute swáy,
And grow wíser and bétter as lífe wears awáy.    *Dr. Pope.*

In this measure a syllable is often retrenched from the first foot, as

Diógenes súrly and próud.    *Dr. Pope.*

When présent, we lóve, and when ábsent agrée,
I thínk not of Íris, nor Íris of me.    *Dryden.*

These measures are varied by many combinations, and sometimes by double endings, either with or without rhyme, as in the heroick measure.

'Tis the divinity that stirs *within us*,
'Tis heaven itself that points out *an hereafter*,
And intimates eternity to man.    *Addison.*

So in that of eight syllables,

They neither added nor confounded,
They neither wanted nor abounded.    *Prior.*

In that of seven,

For resistance I could fear none,
  But with twenty ships had done,
What thou, brave and happy Vernon,
  Hast atchiev'd with six alone.     *Glover.*

In that of six,

'Twas when the seas were roaring,
  With hollow blasts of wind,
A damsel lay deploring,
  All on a rock reclin'd.     *Gay.*

In the anapestick,

When terrible tempests assail us.
  And mountainous billows affright,
Nor power nor wealth can avail us,
  But skilful industry steers right.     *Ballad.*

To these measures and their laws, may be reduced every species of English verse.

Our versification admits of few licences, except a *synalœpha*, or elision of *e* in *the* before a vowel, as *th' eternal*; and more rarely of *o* in *to*, as *t' accept*; and a *synaresis*, by which two short vowels coalesce into one syllable, as *question, special*; or a word is contracted by the expulsion of a short vowel before a liquid, as *av'rice, temp'rance*.

Thus have I collected rules and examples, by which the English language may be learned, if the reader be already acquainted with grammatical terms, or taught by a master to those that are more ignorant. To have written a grammar for such as are not yet initiated in the schools, would have been tedious, and perhaps at last ineffectual.